YOU *already* ARE

WRITTEN BY M.H. CLARK

DESIGNED BY JUSTINE EDGE

YOU HAVE A LIFETIME OF PRACTICE
SEEING THE BEAUTY IN EVERYONE ELSE.

YOU HAVE A LIFETIME OF PRACTICE
NOTICING WHAT IS WHOLE AND WONDERFUL
AND WORTHWHILE IN OTHERS.

WHAT IF, FOR THIS MOMENT, YOU
TURNED YOUR FOCUS TOWARDS YOU?

WHAT IF YOU TOOK A LITTLE TIME
TO LET YOUR EYES ADJUST TO THE
BRILLIANCE THAT IS YOURS?

YOU MIGHT FIND THAT YOU ARE
MUCH MORE THAN YOU HAVE BEEN
GIVING YOURSELF CREDIT FOR.

YOU MIGHT FIND THAT YOU ARE
FILLED WITH THE GOOD THINGS
YOU SEE IN EVERYONE ELSE.

AND YOU MIGHT FIND, TO YOUR
SURPRISE, THAT SO MANY OF THE
THINGS YOU HOPE TO BE ARE THINGS

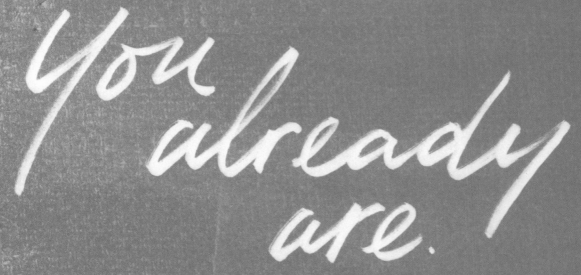

You already are.

NO, YOU WILL NEVER BE PERFECTLY PERFECT.
BUT YOU WILL BE INCREDIBLY, STRIKINGLY,
HEART-SWELLINGLY WONDERFUL.

YOU WILL BE A HUMAN BEING WHO IS
DOING EVERYTHING YOU CAN WITH
EVERYTHING YOU HAVE.

YOU WILL BE A HUMAN BEING WHO IS
GETTING BETTER AT THE WORK AND
THE CHALLENGE OF LIFE.

YOU WILL BE A HUMAN BEING WHO
TAKES WHAT YOU ARE GIVEN AND MAKES
SOMETHING REMARKABLE WITH IT.

IN FACT,

You alrea

dly are.

YOU
ALREADY
ARE

MADE OF EVERYTHING

YOU'LL NEED TO MEET

THE WORK THAT'S

AHEAD OF YOU.

YOU
ALREADY
ARE

ON YOUR WAY
TO THE NEXT
SMALL WONDER,
THE NEXT
BRIGHT MOMENT,
THE NEXT
GOOD THING.

WHEN YOU F

WISHING YOU

ENOUGH TO

DAY, FEEL YOU

BEATING, STE

AT THE CENTE

REMEMBER: Y

ND YOURSELF

WERE **STRONG**

HANDLE THIS

R OWN HEART

ADY AND SURE

R OF YOU, AND

already are.

WHEN YOU FIND YOU HAVE FORGOTTEN

your spark,

REMEMBER THAT ANY TIME YOU WANT,

YOU CAN GO TO THE MIRROR AND FIND IT IN

your eyes.

AND WHEN YOU ARE TIRED,
REMEMBER IT IS BECAUSE
YOU ARE WORKING HARD.

AND WHEN YOU ARE LONELY,
REMEMBER IT IS BECAUSE
**YOU KNOW THE KIND OF
LOVE YOU NEED.**

AND WHEN YOU ARE
CONTENT, REMEMBER TO
LET YOURSELF BE.

AND WHEN YOU ARE
FULL OF JOY, REMEMBER
YOU DESERVE THIS.

YOU ALREADY ARE
SO MUCH OF WHAT
YOU WANT TO BECOME.
THE SEED TO ALL THAT

growth

IS IN YOU.

YOU
ALREADY
ARE

YOUR OWN ANSWER

TO EVERY QUESTION,

YOUR OWN PATH

TO THE FUTURE,

YOUR OWN LIGHT

ALONG THE WAY.

THE LITTLE VOICE
IN YOUR HEART
ALREADY KNOWS
WHAT'S TRUE.
AND YOU ALREADY
KNOW HOW TO

hear it.

AND IF YOU HAVE

FORGOTTEN YOUR

OWN CAPABILITY,

REMEMBER THAT YOUR

BODY AND YOUR SPIRIT

HAVE CARRIED YOU

THROUGH SO MUCH

ALREADY—AND THAT

THEY WANT TO

continue.

AND IF YOU HA

YOUR OWN CAPA

THAT ALL THE **LO**

CHALLENGE, AL

ALL THE **WORK**

HELD ARE A **PAR**

AND THAT THEF

VE FORGOTTEN
CITY, REMEMBER
VE AND ALL THE
L THE **JOY** AND
OU HAVE EVER
T **OF YOU** STILL.
E IS ROOM FOR

more.

REMEMBER TO LOVE THE

SO MUCH YOU ALREADY ARE,

AS YOU BUILD TOWARDS THE

SO MUCH YOU ARE

becoming.

REMEMBER TO SEE THE

good

THAT IS IN YOU, THE WAY
YOU SEE IT IN OTHERS.

REMEMBER THAT LIFE IS

beautiful

AND IT IS HARD, AND

YOU GET BETTER AT IT.

REMEMBER THAT

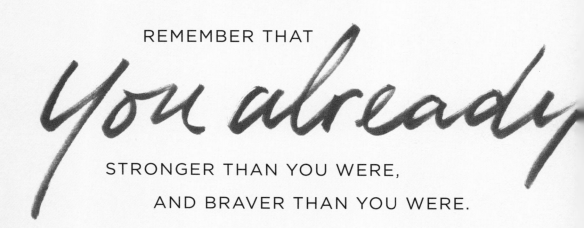
You already

STRONGER THAN YOU WERE,

AND BRAVER THAN YOU WERE.

YOU HAVE ALREADY

FOUND THE

wisdom

THAT IS YOURS,

AND PUT IT TO WORK.

You a

ARE TRANSI

THE WORLD

WAY INTO

AND BEAUTY, A

already

ORMING WHAT
SENDS YOUR
ERSPECTIVE,
ND **SUBSTANCE.**

AND NO, YOU ARE NOT
ALL THE WAY THERE.
BUT YOU ARE CLOSER.

AND NO, YOU ARE
NOT YET FINISHED.
**BUT LOOK HOW FAR YOU
HAVE ALREADY COME.**

AND AS YOU MOV
THE YEARS UN
A **FULLER** VER
VERSION, A **TRU**
THE SELF YOU'
REMEMBER: **YOU**
THIS *Won*

FORWARD, AS

OLD YOU INTO

ON, A **CLEARER**

ER VERSION OF

MEANT TO BE,

ALWAYS WERE

derful.

YOU ARE HERE TO DO
INCREDIBLE THINGS.
BRAVE THINGS.
BOLD THINGS.
THINGS THAT ONLY
YOU CAN DO.
YOU ARE HERE TO BE
A LITTLE BIT OF A

Miracle.

AND THE TRUTH IS,

You alre

ady are.

COMPENDIUM®

live inspired

WRITTEN BY: M.H. CLARK

DESIGNED BY: JUSTINE EDGE

EDITED BY: AMELIA RIEDLER

Photography Credits:
Pages 8, 9: Akotography / istockphoto.com; pages 16, 17, 28, 29: NNehring / istockphoto.com; pages 18, 19: Toltek / istockphoto.com; pages 26, 27: Cecile Hournau / unsplash.com; pages 30, 31: Oksix / creativemarket.com; pages 32, 33: PeskyMonkey / istockphoto.com; pages 40, 41: Mommuth / istockphoto.com; pages 44, 45: Melpomenem / istockphoto.com; pages 46, 47: Jonathan Knepper / unsplash.com

Library of Congress Control Number: 2017958766 | ISBN: 978-1-946873-00-2

4th printing. Printed in China with soy inks on FSC®-Mix certified paper.

Create meaningful moments with gifts that inspire.

CONNECT WITH US
live-inspired.com | sayhello@compendiuminc.com

@compendiumliveinspired
#compendiumliveinspired